Write History

JP ROBINSON

"Anybody can make history. Only a great man can write it." —Oscar Wilde

About the Author

Author, teacher, historian and international speaker, JP Robinson began writing as a teen for a newspaper in New York and won local recognition for his literary works. His historical fiction novels are high-adrenaline plots laced with unexpected twists.

Connect with JP, get exclusive access to deals and more via his website: **www.jprobinsonbooks.com**.

Friend JP. Search "JPRobinsonBooks" on any of the following social media platforms.

What readers are saying:

"I would highly recommend it *[Twiceborn]* to anyone, but especially to those who enjoy historical fiction."—Maureen

"I was about to set it *[Bride Tree]* down for the night but then found that I couldn't. His spiritual angle was spot on!"—A.M. Heath, Author of *Ancient Words*

"My first thought upon finishing it *[Bride Tree]* was: 'Wow!'"—Emma

"I recommend *Bride Tree* to adults who like to be emotionally gripped by a book and who enjoy a book that keeps you turning pages— a book you just can't put down."—Kelly

"*[In the Shadow of Your Wings]* Fantastic WWI historical fiction book. Fast paced, you won't want to put this book down. Great story, characters and believable. Looking forward to reading more of the *Northshire Heritage* series. Wish they were available now."—Caroline

WORKSHOP-IN-YOUR-POCKET

Write History

JP ROBINSON

Table of Contents

Introduction

In 2017, I found myself at a Barnes and Noble book signing, right next to a woman who writes murder novels. You know, the kind of person that looks at a tombstone and says, "I feel inspired!"

Hmm....

Anyway, a prospective customer walked over to her table. The author introduced herself and, while slanting a glance that dripped morbid humor in the customer's direction, she whispered, "I kill people… tastefully."

Shudder.

The customer acknowledged this comment with a polite nod then came over to my booth. "And what do you do?" Curiosity tinged her voice.

With a smile, I held up a copy of *Twiceborn*, and replied, "She kills people, but I bring the dead back to life!"

That is the power granted to historical authors. We are gifted with both an opportunity *and* responsibility to resurrect the people, places and times that have shaped the world. If you're an author who writes about the past, history is your passion.

Regardless of your preferred genre—historical fiction, biographies or memoirs, to name a few—resurrecting the past is an art that only dedicated, talented authors can do with grace.

Moses, Joan of Arc and millions of others wrote history, but these iconic figures and more all need *you* to write *their* story.

As you peruse the following pages and immerse yourself in the included exercises, adapt the following principles to your own genre and create a tantalizing portrayal of the events that have shaped our world.

I conduct writing seminars in various parts of the country and have realized that there's simply never enough time to do justice to each topic. So, I've put it together in a book that you can reference time and again. It's formatted to give you the workshop experience but includes more detailed information that you can peruse at your own pace.

At the end of each chapter, I've included a short synopsis of the main points as well as questions tailored to take your manuscript to the next level.

Ready for it?

I think you are.

Write history. Write well. Write now.

JP Robinson

CHAPTER 1:

Why write history?

Many people dream of making history but it's actually more enjoyable to write about it than to make it. For example, it's better to write about Julius Caesar than it is to be Julius Caesar. I mean, you know how his story ends.

So, what qualifies as history?

Merriam-Webster gives a litany of descriptions that essentially revolve around events in the past. When writing, however, we want to move beyond the literal definition. In terms of this guide, I define historical as having taken place at least 50 years in the past.

Needless to say, this is very subjective and there are always exceptions but, as an author of history, you want to bear two things in mind:

1. Does the event you are writing about have a national, societal or global impact? Basically, is it important enough to qualify as being "history-making?"
2. Is it far enough removed from the present that *readers* will see it as a historical event?

For example, writing a book about Starbucks's

newest latte would not qualify as historical. While it *is* radically important—at least in my mind—a new type of latte does *not* have a significant enough global or societal impact to qualify as a historical event. Also, it's probably too close to the present for your readers to buy in.

Events such as the American Civil War or the reign of Genghis Khan are great examples of historical events. They take us to places and people far beyond our lifespan and, as such, definitely qualify as being *historical.*

Writing about the past involves a lot of sweat and blood—most of it the blood of other people, thankfully—but a good bit of it will be yours (metaphorically speaking!). To the warriors, politicians and monarchs of the past fell the duty of shaping history but your challenge is to:

- Recreate an authentic, believable world
- Accurately portray realistic, multi-dimensional people that reflect the mindsets of their time
- Depict clothing, accents, weapons and other accoutrements of your chosen era
- Weave an enthralling story that will keep readers wanting more
- Educate your readers without making your book a textbook

… and the list goes on. Doubtless, you can come up with a few more. In short, writing about the past is in itself a challenge but it is well worth it. Here's why:

1. Times may change but people do not.

The present mirrors the past in a plenary of

ways. We may have different technologies and social attitudes than our predecessors on this planet but, at heart, humans remain remarkably stagnant. Jealousy, greed, infidelity, ambition and all the other elements that make up a gripping plot remain alive and well within the heart of humanity.

Therefore, writers of history automatically start off with an advantage that writers of other genres may *not* have. From the first page, you are gifted with the mixed blessing of relatable characters. You may not have sloughed through the mud of Passchendaele, Belgium with the soldiers of the First World War, but you *have* felt fear. As have millions of others.

Our response to circumstances is strikingly similar to those of previous generations. Imitation is embedded in our genetic code. As a society, we form social idols, we let fashion and the opinions of celebrities guide our actions exactly as previous civilizations have done for millennia.

So when you pick up your pen—or your laptop—remember that you're writing to an audience who is presently living what the characters in your book have already experienced. What an opportunity to educate, to share powerful lessons!

2. People read to learn.

A recent study conducted by author/researcher M.K. Tod (AWriterofHistory.com) of over 2,400 historical fiction readers found that about 57 percent of readers frequently or always pick up a book to learn, while a whopping 70 percent frequently or always read to appreciate other places.

Be it scorching sands of the Sahara or the luxuries of Luxemburg, readers are eager to engage in alternative places and epochs. As authors, we can provide them with a round-trip ticket anywhere that our inner muse has already taken us.

3. Authors can set current social issues against the backdrop of historical contexts

We say that history is flawed but so is the present. As such, effective writers of the past can do more than transport readers into the past.

An effective writer of history is empowered to teach life-altering truths through the characters he or she creates. You can either spell out the issue to your reader and place it in a historical context or, if the similarity is blatant enough, you can create an allegory.

Whether you're targeting injustice, religious freedom or are addressing more personal concerns such as substance abuse, there are plenty of historical opportunities that can serve as a backdrop to whatever point you're trying to make.

In 2016 I launched a series called *Secrets of Versailles.* As a teacher of French history, yes, I confess that I wanted to share the intricate twists of the Bourbon dynasty with my readers, but I also had other, more subtle goals.

High on the list was to illustrate the irreparable hurt caused by infidelity. The web of characters portrayed this truth in undeniable black-and-white while offering a viable means of emotional recovery for readers who may have endured such an experience.

For memoir and autobiographical writers, the need for historical writing is even clearer. Capturing the raw thoughts and ideas of previous generations sets the stage for learning and exposure without the layers of plot, emotional description and character development in fiction that can obscure the point you're trying to make.

But even more important is the fact that biographies and memoirs allow authors to tell real stories that inspire. History is made by men and women whose stories are moving. Their voices may be silent, but, through you, they can relay the most powerful moments of their lives to another generation.

Convinced?

Awesome.

Now let's get to the good stuff.

Takeaway:

To be considered historical, the event should have taken place **at least 50 years ago** and/or should be of significant societal importance.

Four of the many reasons to write about the past include:

- Times change but people don't

- People read to learn

- Authors can present current social issues against the backdrop of historical contexts

- To tell a story of personal struggle and triumph

Personal Reflection:

1. Why do you write? Sum your reasons up in 10 words or less.

2. Think about the piece you are currently writing, have finished writing, or are about to write. What is your primary goal in drafting your manuscript? Your secondary goal?

   a. To transport readers to another time/ place
   b. To educate readers about an important event(s)

    c. To set a current social issue against a historical context
    d. To inspire someone to follow in the footsteps of greatness

3. As a *reader* of historical books, what is your primary reason for picking up a novel or non-fiction piece?

    a. To learn
    b. To visit other places
    c. Another reason

CHAPTER 2:

Setting the stage

One of my favorite paintings is an impressionist work by Claude Monet of his wife and son while on a stroll. It's called *Woman with Parasol.*

There are many things that transform this ordinary moment into an unforgettable masterpiece, but I'd like to point your attention to the one thing we all see but probably do not notice: **the background.**

If Monet had opted to paint a stormy sky with lowering gray clouds, or if he had thrown Madame Monet into a tropical locale, replete with mangoes and swinging monkeys, the simple elegance of this scene would be irrevocably lost. It is the serene energy of the scudding clouds and bright sky that allow us to focus on the three principal objects: the woman, her son and the parasol.

I like to compare the setting of a book to the backdrop of any painting. **The backdrop must serve to enhance the focal point(s) of the actual text—the characters and the plot.**

You, the author, should be very particular when building your literary backdrop as it will guide your research, set the overall pace for your novel and can have a major impact on your readers' ability to connect with your characters.

What actually makes up a book's setting?

This question is a bit subjective, but I think it's important for you to have a clear understanding of what I mean when I use this word. Simply put, the setting is everything except the plot and the characters themselves. To be a bit more specific, I've streamlined the idea of *setting* into five broad categories.

Consider each of these categories very carefully when crafting your setting while taking into consideration the starter thoughts below.

Location	Epoch	Time Duration	Spoken Language	Culture
Where is my plot taking place?	What era do I want to depict?	What time span will my novel cover?	Do your characters speak English? If so, is there a dialect?	Every-thing else that makes us human.

Location:

Location, location, location! It's important in real estate, but it's critical for a novel.

Where your story takes place is almost as important as *what* takes place in your story. You'll choose your location based on the story that you want to tell. Some historical novels are fixed in one place, however, it is common to see both novels and biographies moving between multiple locations depending on the context of the novel.

For historical fiction authors, the geography, climate and regional history will determine a logical reaction of your character to a crisis. This leads to some pretty interesting research.

Fun fact: did you know that in the United Kingdom, it's not uncommon to leave sheep outside in winter?

"Why this random factoid?" you ask.

Well, it proves my point.

In the final book of *Northshire Heritage*, I had my protagonist coming home in winter with sheep happily saying "baa" as they pawed through the snow on a hillock looking for grass.

When I reread the scene, I thought, *wait a second. That's impossible. Sheep will be in a barn or manger, not on a hill!* Well, geography is everything. A little research and I learned something new. European shepherds (mainly in the UK) actually do often leave their sheep outside. Again, location is everything.

For non-fiction writing, things are a little more rigid. You are more focused on facts and analysis. Your writing may focus more on *how* the location impacted the protagonist's life than anything else. For example, how did the fact that Hitler was born in Austria-Hungary and not Germany impact his political and social worldview? Did it play any part at all?

When weaving in this layer of your setting, do not succumb to the temptation of focusing on the country. You also want to pay a good bit of attention to the physical structures that your characters inhabit.

Be sure to consider things like the age of buildings and how they looked during the period in which you are writing. Take into consideration what roads existed (or did not exist).

For example, if you are looking at a map of London's East End, be sure that you're describing it as it *was* at the time you are writing and not as it *is*. Google maps is a great tool but try to corroborate the buildings and data you draw from it *now* with data that would have existed *then*.

Consider using photos or drawings of structures taken or made during your time period. Which is the perfect segway into our next component.

Epoch:

Choose your epoch based on the theme that you want to project to your audience. Remember I said that effective historical authors teach something through their writing? Well, nothing gives you a platform from which you can project your message like the chosen epoch.

If you're writing about civil rights, for example, it might be better to set your story during the 60's or latter half of the 20th century than during an era such as the American Revolution. True, you can still get your point across when writing in a different time period, but it won't be as effective.

The theme is reflected in the times.

In other words, whatever message you want to project to your audience should be *lived* by the protagonists and antagonists in that era.

Please note that, when writing Christian historical fiction, the epoch isn't as important as it is with other forms of historical literature. This is simply because the main themes that are often depicted in Christian historical fiction can be applied across the ages.

Forgiveness, sacrifice, the power of faith etc. are timeless principles that men and women have exemplified throughout history.

Time duration:

It's really important to determine how much time will elapse in your fiction or non-fiction piece. Not only will this help you develop realistic character arcs, but it will let you know how much detail to include in each chapter.

As an author, you need to decide if you're going to cover the entire Great Depression or only three years of it. This might depend on whether you're writing a stand-alone manuscript or a series. If you're writing Biblical fiction, will you detail the entire ministry of Jesus Christ or only the days before His crucifixion?

If you're a writer of historical works, you're probably also a reader of the same and, as such, I'm going to guess that you're familiar with datelines. Datelines are critical because they help readers keep pace with the story and give clear evidence for the story's time duration. True, some readers skim over them, but they can help us pace our story effectively.

Spoken Language:

Got dialect? Obviously, the language you choose will be reflected in your location. Also obvious is the fact that, no matter where your story takes place, it will be written in English.

But, even though your manuscript is written in English, most people don't think about dialect. Make sure your characters' dialects are their own… and not yours. They might all speak English but—to make them 3D—be sure that their version of English reflects both their heritage and their location.

If you're writing about a place that doesn't speak English, sprinkle in a few foreign words that suit the plot and context just to give your book a little more authenticity. You can have some fun with this. British English is very different than American in some ways and linguistic misunderstandings are a great way to "lighten up" a story. But if you put in foreign words or use an atypical English dialect, be sure your readers can follow along. *Capiche?*

Culture:

I grew up in New York and we used to call it a melting pot. Now, I think they describe it as a salad bowl to be politically correct (hysterical, I know). It's still a melting pot to me, by the way, and that's because the fusion of different cultures made the entire New York experience unique.

The cultural aspect of your novel is your proverbial melting pot. Here is where every other aspect of your character's life gets melded together into a plot that's uniquely yours.

Things like religion, music, dress code, hairstyles, weapons, slang and dozens of other aspects of human life should all be reflected in the setting.

Don't be overwhelmed: you can do this! You just need to weave in little tidbits here and there.

Fun fact: *Marie Antoinette's celebrated hairstyle was called le pouf. She wore it with a wooden battleship woven within to celebrate a French naval victory.*

Women, imitating the queen's style, went on a fashion craze, in some cases ruining their fortunes and relationships.

Weaving snippets of information like this into your plot, easily gives the reader an idea of the culture. In this case, a fashion craze led to excessive spending. Hm… has anything changed?

In reality, a dozen authors can write about the same historical event but, by simply changing the background, the reader will walk away with an entirely different picture (or perspective) each time. And *that* my friend, is the beauty of our gift.

Takeaway:

1. Your setting is everything but the plot and characters.
2. The book's setting must enhance the plot and its characters.
3. Pay special attention to the five elements above (location, epoch, time duration, language and culture)

Personal Reflection:

1. Again focus on a current, past or future manuscript. Have you clearly identified the setting? If so, what tweaks will you make to your setting after reading this chapter?
2. Diagram the setting of said manuscript below. Use a separate piece of paper for more space.

Setting: Think: **LETSC** (Let's see! Get it?)	My **L**ocation is:	
	My **E**poch is:	
	My book lasts for (**T**ime **S**equence/Duration):	
	The **C**ultural aspects I'll include are:	

CHAPTER 3:

The "Write" setting

There are two main questions to keep in mind when setting the stage.

1. What will keep readers turning pages?
2. What do I already know/can I learn a lot about?

Historical authors keep readers engaged by weaving an irresistible plot in an era with which the reader may or may not be familiar. This is both a blessing and a curse (more on that later).

To choose the best setting for your novel or biography, you must always remember to **P.R.A.E.**

P: Is there a problem going on in society at that time?

R: Is that problem relatable? Can contemporary readers connect/understand that problem?

A: Are you an expert on that era?

E: Is that era exciting?

Let's break this down a little further.

Problem:

Winston Churchill is often believed to have said,

"never let a good crisis go to waste."

Whether Churchill actually *did* say this and what exactly he meant by it aren't really important for our purposes. What *is* important is the fact that... he's right! Crisis is one of the keys to choosing a powerful, emotionally-compelling era.

To hook your readers, remember this key concept: *hard times are king.*

Some part of our inner psyche likes tough times... for other people, of course. As a society, we're currently facing difficult realities thus it is easy for us to empathize with characters who are struggling to carve out an existence in the face of religious persecution, financial meltdowns, war, or social injustice.

Place your story against a compelling backdrop of a regional or global challenge and you'll pique your reader's interest. Neglect to do so and you risk your book never being read.

Let's compare two scenarios:

Setting A:

A beautiful, raven-haired shepherdess watches her flock from her perch on a gently sloping hill. Green grass, on which dewdrops dance in the brilliant sunlight and azure skies, wave sleepily in the gentle breeze which wafts down from the lofty distant mountains.

Setting B:

The dark skies above Sussex County belied the fact that the New Year had come. No fireworks illuminated the darkness for fear that the German zeppelins would drop their own firepower on those who watched from the ground. Instead of joyfully proclaiming the hope of a new beginning, church bells tolled an incessant dirge for the dead. (Extract from *In the Shadow of Your Wings*)

I don't know about you, but the first scenario almost makes my eyes want to join the green grass in their sleepy waving! In the second excerpt, I take the first step in hooking my readers. I also give myself room for "plot play," or the manipulation of my character's life set against the backdrop of real events to show personal growth.

For example, *In the Shadow of Your Wings* presents us with Leila, a German spy sent to infiltrate the home of a British government figure. When Leila falls in love with her target, things get rather interesting. As Churchill insinuated, there is a crisis—a world war in this case—which paves the way for a gripping plot. The reader wants to know if Leila will betray her country or the man she loves. Will he ever find out who she is? If so, how will their ensuing marriage survive?

Infuse history but if you're writing fiction, be sure not to let the historical events dominate each page. Avoid "textbook" syndrome but weave a story around the facts. More on this in <u>Chapter 5: Hook your reader's emotions.</u>

When determining what epoch your book will call home, be sure it is a time period that already has at least one major crisis. In so doing, you give yourself room to toss your lasso around your reader's heart and pull him along for an unforgettable ride.

On that note, I have another word of caution. Too much tension can overwhelm some readers, so be careful not to throw too much at them at once.

I've been guilty of doing that to my readers. It's one thing to hook them but quite another to have them dying of anxiety on the couch! (That's never really happened. At least… not as far as I know for sure.) Ahem… Moving on!

Relatable:

Let's be honest. As a society, we're self-obsessed. (Selfies, anyone?) The "selfie" concept carries over to literature. We love characters and situations that are similar to our own. That's one of the things that makes a book sell.

Everyone wants a character, setting, and experiences that are at least vaguely similar to their own life story. This is why many historical novels often portray situations in which women are dissatisfied with their social status, characters are connected to blended families, or nations are ripped apart by religious conflict. These are concepts that we understand.

As an author, you need to choose an era that offers the potential for relatability. It's not enough to have a problem—you need a problem with which your readers can emotionally identify.

To make your characters relatable, think beyond the scope of your own life.

Think outside *your* box as you breathe life into your characters. This is hard to do because, again, we're all self-centered by nature to a certain degree. Authors need to create circumstances that confront others within society. Don't be afraid to tackle tough issues that society skirts, such as abuse, racism or suicide. There *are* people out there who experience whatever you're writing out on a daily basis.

When writing, diversify your character's experiences/background to improve the odds of at least one of them connecting with your readers.

As a teen, I was exposed to a book my sister read called *Redeeming Love* by Francine Rivers. Judging by the cover, I admit it's a girly book, but I had read a few of her "non-girly" books before and so I sneaked this one from my big sis.

Well, I ended up reading the whole thing. Not only did I read it, but I enjoyed it to the extent that it actually impacted my worldview. I mention *Redeeming Love* because the author decided to weave themes of prostitution, child abuse and the quest for love at a risky price, into the larger picture of biblical allegory.

While many of Francine's readers probably haven't walked the streets, perhaps they can connect to the other theme of abuse or fruitless relationships. The male protagonist struggles with his own issues which also increase the relatability odds.

As a guy, I can connect to the male protagonist's frustrations while Francine's female readers will probably empathize with the female lead. The point is, the author varied the major elements of the story so that different readers can see traces of themselves in the characters. You need to do the same.

So how do you do this?

Step out of yourself and focus on the needs, tastes and desires of your target audience (TA). Here are a few solid strategies:

Interview others similar to your TA. Get a general feel for what they like or don't like.

Collect personal stories of friends that you can modify or use as a basis for shaping your *own* characters.

Take your *dislikes* and make them your character's *likes*.

Keep reading. The more stories you encounter, the better stories you'll craft.

People watch: Sit in a café with a newspaper so you don't look too conspicuous. Watch the gestures, actions and facial cues of others around you. Take notes on a piece of paper.

Hey, if you wear dark shades, they might think you're FBI!

Are you an expert on it?

Even more important than crisis, however, is knowledge. Remember I told you that a reader's personal interest in a historical era is both a blessing and a curse? Here's the logic.

Historical readers sometimes read about eras they know well and, other times, they pick up books that detail eras with which they may not be very familiar. Either way, they are counting on *you,* the author, to be the expert. Your novel, biography or memoir must contain facts that will educate as well as entertain.

If you're a history buff, you'll probably read historical books to learn. Now, imagine that you picked up a book about the American Revolution that was written by an author whose entire life was spent in China. Is it possible?

Absolutely.

But the author will have to do a lot of research in order to write convincingly about a major historical event that isn't part of his country's history and he probably isn't, therefore, an expert on the subject or its impact.

If you're writing about an epoch with which you are not intimately familiar, be sure to do research so you can convince readers you're an expert.

How do you know you're an expert? Give yourself the 45 minute test. I use 45 minutes because, as a teacher of language and history, 45 minutes is about the average length of a class. When you're writing, you're teaching… hopefully in a very engaging and fun way.

Test yourself. If you can't talk about a specific topic for 45 minutes without reaching for notes (or Google), you need to do some more research before actively sitting down to write. This rule should be applied to all the major historical components of your manuscript.

There's no shame in not knowing everything about the epoch in which your story will be set. None of us were born omniscient. However, 21st century authors are empowered with tools that our creative ancestors couldn't *dream* of having.

Couple the power of the internet with microfiche records then add video footage of historic events (original or even reenactments) and cap it all off with a tourist-oriented global culture. In short, modern times are a writer's dream.

Research is key. I suggest keeping a research log (a simple Excel spreadsheet or a notepad works fine) in which you approximate how much time you spend researching major themes/topics that will appear in your text. Note that the best research doesn't always take place at a computer. Consider the resources listed in the following chart.

Resource Ideas	Print	Human	Media
Travel/ Life experiences	Newspapers	Friends	Videos
	Diaries/Letters	Family/Co-workers	Music

No matter how you do your research, before you complete your first draft, be sure that you meet the requirements of the 45 minute rule.

Exciting:

Don't give your readers what they can perceive as a list of facts. If they wanted raw history, they'd have picked up a textbook! Instead, they chose to read *your* book. And that's something you should feel proud about.

But be respectful of your reader's time. Choose historical moments that allow for dramatic tension, romance and political manipulation. Like succulent grapes on a sun-kissed vine, history is ripe with opportune moments. You just have to pick one.

Takeaway:

1. Keep the following 2 points in mind when setting up your novel:
   a. What will keep my reader turning pages?
   b. What do I already know/can I learn a lot about?
2. Hard times are king.
3. Don't forget to PRAE.
   - **P:** Problem
   - **R:** Relatable
   - **A:** Are you an expert on the topic?
   - **E:** Is the time period exciting?

Personal Reflection:

1. How doeoes your chosen setting meet the PRAE requirements outlined above?

2. Pick one protagonist from your novel. On a separate sheet of paper, do a scatter diagram (modeled on next page) that shows how your character can be relatable to your TA.

List the character's roles then include a short description of the major problems he/she faces. Are those issues common to many people?

Repeat this activity with your other characters including the antagonist(s).

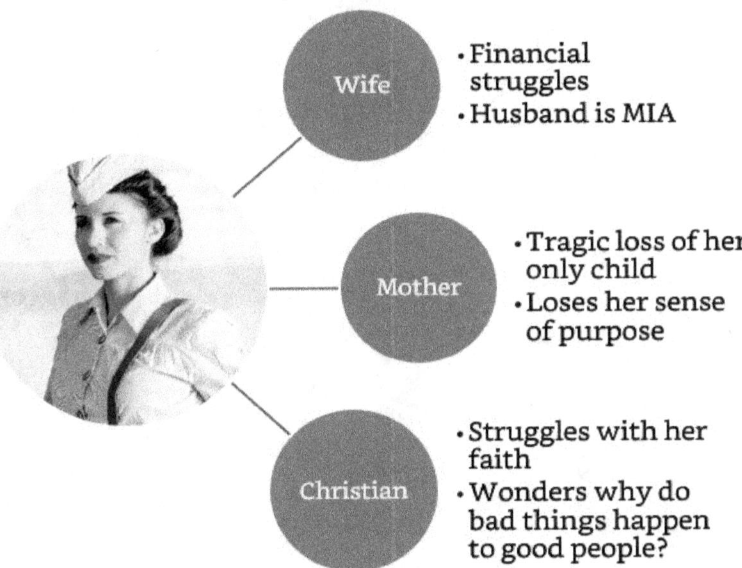

CHAPTER 4:

Creating authentic, 3D characters

At the beginning of our journey, I mentioned that the point of being a historical author is to bring the dead to life. There's no better way to do this than to create characters who virtually walk off the page. It's not enough to have a killer plot; you need to be able to connect with your character and, in so doing, infuse him or her with an ability to live in the imaginations of your readers.

As you flesh out your characters, keep the following components at the forefront of your thoughts:

1. Knowing your characters
2. Descriptive details
3. Thinking past your own perspectives

Knowing your characters

So... I've got bad news. There's an affliction that's common to all professional writers called *Crazy Author Syndrome*. It sneaks up on you, probably after you've written between 50-100,000 words of prose. Here are some of the most common symptoms:

- Talking about your characters at random moments, regardless of where you might be

- Asking others questions like, "What do you think *Leila* **{insert your own character name here}** is doing right now?"

- Bursting out laughing while others are discussing something serious because your character just said a hilarious joke that no one but you can hear.

Do you get my point?

---

*Before your characters can be real to your readers, they must first be real to **you**.*

3D characters aren't so much the product of gifted writing as they are the product of thorough description. Too often, writers get lost in the jungle of creating compelling plots and lose sight of the fact that readers need a clear picture of *who* the characters are.

Here again, good research will help you develop a holistic picture that is essential to creating a "living" character. Historical writers are either writing about *real* people or fictional people in *real* situations.

In either case, you want to spend a good bit of time researching a person similar to your guy/gal.

Let's take Maximilien Robespierre for example, the antagonist of *Bride Tree*. Robespierre was a real person who was pretty much responsible for the Reign of Terror—an unfortunate consequence of the French Revolution.

When drafting *Bride Tree*, I became intrigued by the man who was known as "The Incorruptible" among France's commoners. This same man later contributed to the death of at least 17,000 people during the Reign of Terror, many of them those same commoners whose cause he had once defended. What caused such a radical change? Was their any indication of his murderous nature in childhood?

Research led me to unearthing childhood descriptions of Robespierre by his close relatives and peers. Bloodlines and descriptions of the temperament of his parents were all clues that slowly allowed me to piece together a picture of a man who literally became the master of life and death—at least until the pendulum of public opinion swung against him.

If you're creating a fictional character in a real setting, you want to research a *real* person in that time period. Don't just learn that person's story; study his or her habits, religious beliefs and clothing. Investigate what others had to say about his or her private life.

Small, unexplored details can help you develop a complete picture of your character that will make him or her real to *you*. So **dig, dig, dig.** Consider yourself an investigative journalist who's unafraid to ask the important questions.

Someone out there has the answers.

Once the characters are real in your mind, you'll be better prepared to write about them authentically. Beyond research, consider the following techniques:

1. Pretend your character has been caught doing something illegal and put him or her on trial.

   Play the role of both prosecution and defense attorney and jot down whatever you discover about your character's personality or past life.

2. Describe your character(s) to someone who knows nothing about your manuscript.

3. Create a visual web/grid detailing your character(s) personality.

4. Find a headshot of someone that represents your character(s). While staring at his/her face, brainstorm all the personality traits that come to mind.

5. Write a diary/journal of your characters daily experiences. Be sure that these have little to do with your plot.

Descriptive details:

"The big door of history turns on small hinges."—Unknown

Of course, the authenticity of your characters will be undergirded by your plot to a certain degree. But, even more importantly, the subtle details are the attributes that give a character a shadow.

Remember: **it's all in the details.**

Details are the small things that are often overlooked by authors. It's so easy to get caught up in the fact that our protagonist is shooting someone that we neglect to mention the type of gun he uses.

But when we fail to mention the nuances of a scene, we lose out on its true power to impact our reader. You can choose to say, "she pulled up in a silver car" or "she pulled up in a silver Ferrari." The simple detail that has been slipped in makes a world of difference and effortlessly gives a lot more information to the reader.

Which leads us to another point.

Details shouldn't be fired at the reader. This kind of writing slows down the overall pace of your manuscript and can be a source of frustration. Rather, details should be cleanly inserted.

Instead of telling us that your character "glanced at his watch" have him "glance at his Rolex," or, by contrast, "at the shattered face of a too-small wrist-watch."

The same concept can be applied to historical writing. Use details that will give non-intrusive support for the character you're trying to flesh out. Consider the following when writing:

- **Your character's vocabulary**
Would he use words like "ring" instead of "to telephone" for example?

- **Your character's clothing:**
If she's conservative, would her skirt be knee-length or lower?

- **Physical structures accessible to your character:**
Would your character look at his or her reflection in a mirror or a puddle?

Never make assumptions. Just because *you* have easy access to a functioning toilet and running water, don't assume that your character does. When in doubt, it is always best to do your research, so you don't inadvertently place your character in an

impossible situation.

See past your own perspectives

Americans have often been accused of being detached from reality and, to a large degree, this is true. The privileges that have been afforded to the Western world, particularly the United States, have engendered a sort of myopic view that distorts our understanding of history.

This is reflected in many forms of entertainment and you, as an author, have to make the personal choice whether you intend to cater to popular trends or truly "resurrect the past" by your writing.

The heart of good historical writing is to capture the attitudes, tastes and social perspectives of those living in the given times. Capturing these aspects is, in my opinion, even more important than the actual facts.

For example, consider the shift in the social attitudes toward women throughout the last millennium. It is unreasonable to assume that women in the 15th century had the same social perspectives as women in the 21st century. Frankly, history records the lives of many women (such as Suzanna Wesley) who did *not* challenge social norms but lived contented lives as wives and mothers.

The point is, do not *assume* that your perspectives are the same as those who lived before us. Doing so imposes our opinions upon those who are no longer alive to speak for themselves. We rob them of their voice and present to the public a twisted reality.

To carry this thought just a little farther, we all—hopefully—consider the Nazi party to be in the wrong in their treatment of the Jewish people. However, if you are writing a scene that involves a Nazi officer who is part of Himmler's Final Solution, you *need* to get into that man's ideology in order to present a 3D character to your audience unless you deliberately want to make your character atypical to his/her social .

Your perspective and my perspective condemn his attitude. However, in the mind of the character, anti-Semitic actions are acceptable and the norm. Therefore you, the author, need to see past your own perspectives when writing scenes in that character's point of view. In so doing, you will be better able to make your character convincing.

Takeaway:

1. Your characters have to be real to *you* before they can be real to someone else. Think *Crazy Author Syndrome.*
2. Build a complete profile by:
    a. Researching people who surrounded your protagonist (family, friend, etc.)
    b. Putting your character in awkward/interesting situations that have nothing to do with your plot.
    c. Be sure that you are not incarnating yourself in your character. Make him/her have different likes/dislikes than yourself.
3. Weave details into your plot via description.
4. Be sure your character has a mindset that is suited to the times.

Personal Reflection:

1. Pick an antagonist from your cast of characters. Ask yourself, what would you have to change to make him/her a *protagonist*? Make a list of the necessary changes.

2. Pick a minor character in your plot. Conduct an imaginary interview to gain this minor character's perspectives about what's going on in your story. Record yourself asking (and answering) the questions.

3. Create a T-diagram with your own traits on one side and your protagonists character traits on the other. How similar are you? Is there a good degree of difference?

4. Do the same activity but this time, compare two *protagonists* (if there is more than one) in your story. Compare physical, emotional and personality traits. Are there enough differences that will be obvious to your reader?

CHAPTER 5:

Hook your reader's emotions

George Washington is commonly quoted as having compared government to fire. "A useful servant but a dangerous master."

I like to think of emotions in the same way. Emotions—or the lack of them— are at the heart of almost every choice we make. If left uncontrolled, we'll get burned.

As authors, we often focus on our *characters'* emotions, but I argue that our readers' emotions are equally important. The feelings—or again, the *lack* of feelings— your words arouse, will cause readers to make the following choices:

- To continue reading or to stop
- To leave a good review or a negative one
- To purchase your next book or to forgo it

Authors need to get the emotions of their readers under their own control. Obviously, this is never fully possible; readers approach books with various preconceived notions and different world views. But as much as is humanly possible, we want to hook that incredible part of the human spirit that makes us feel.

But how?

I'll answer with another question: Have you watched the news lately? Read trending tweets on Twitter? Seen pictures of your friends on Instagram?

If you answered *yes* to any or all of the above, I have no doubt that you experienced several powerful emotions.

From anger to sympathy to happiness, human emotion is triggered by something that we perceive as REAL.

Readers will feel what you want them to feel if your plot is real to them.

For example, if you've suffered a tragic loss and the protagonist in a book you're reading goes through a similar experience, your own emotions are likely to be hooked as the character regains emotional footing... or not.

Why?

Because it's real to *you*.

This harks back to our segment on relatable writing, but I'd like to go a little deeper at this point.

Relatability isn't enough—you need realism.

You can't know what experiences your readers have lived through but, thankfully, there's a saving grace.

If you make your characters' emotions vivid and their reactions natural, your readers are likely to feel the emotional pull. Deep point of view and character depth will all play into this.

Think back to your favorite book. Chances are you don't just like it because the plot was a winner. You probably think the plot was a winner because your emotions were hooked. Your emotions were hooked because the characters' reactions to tough circumstances were *real.*

Writers of history must make the emotions of people who lived and died centuries ago real to a 21st century reader. Sounds tough?

It is.

But keeping the following tips in mind will help you succeed.

Weave a story around the facts.

Whether you're writing fiction or nonfiction, history is made up of individual stories. Like a patchwork quilt, the life of each person contributes to the fabric of the whole.

The reality is that facts don't pull at our emotions as much as stories do. So make the indisputable facts your anchor points and weave the plot around them. Which leads us to our next point…

Tell us a story not *history*

You want to limit the amount of facts in your novel. After all, you're not writing a textbook! When crafting a biography, you have more leeway with this but remember your audience can only handle so much.

Feel free to twist your plot but avoid bending history too much unless your audience knows that you're writing alternative history. Dramatic changes in the plot give you room to play with your character's emotions and keep them wanting more.

Diversify character profiles

Diversity is the name of the game these days. This doesn't need to be racial diversity if the plot doesn't warrant it. But you can diversify your cast to show different aspects of society. For example, *Bride Tree* centers on the French Revolution, particularly Marie-Antoinette.

Instead of simply alternating between the monarchy and the revolutionaries, I had a lot of fun including the perspectives of the *bourgeois* (the middle class) as well as servants and other people we don't often think about.

We can hook our readers by recreating real emotions that the "minor" characters of history would have felt.

How & why trump what

In most cases, we know the facts. But what tugs at people's emotions is *why* things happened and *how*. Yes, Benedict Arnold betrayed the American revolutionary cause. But *why* he did it is the real question and it's a question that can keep reader   interest.

Historical fiction authors can create fictional stories or reasons around real events. Again, those reasons should reflect the attitudes of the time.

Angela E. Hunt's *Roanoke* provides us with a classic example. Roanoke, also called the Lost Colony, has captivated the imaginations of generations. Hunt's story gives us a plausible reason for the disappearance of about 100 settlers.

Is her story absolute fact?

No.

Is it possible?

Yes.

But while our curiosity might be stirred by the mysterious disappearance, our emotions aren't. What pulls at our hearts is the story that is dramatized in the *how* and *why (speculative)* that the author presents. With real problems and real responses pulling at us, we find ourselves helpless to resist. Again, there isn't a way to guarantee that you'll hook each reader's emotions with every keystroke but the above will definitely improve your chances.

Takeaway:

1. Each reader's emotions are as important to your story as the emotions of your characters.

2. Emotions are triggered by events, memories or scenarios that are real to us as individuals.

3. The more natural your character's reactions are to his or her problems, the more compelling the situation, and the more vivid your character's emotions throughout the manuscript, the more likely you are to hook your readers' emotions.

4. Use the following strategies to help you hook your audience's emotions:
    a. Weave a story around the facts
    b. Tell a story not history.
    c. Diversify your cast of characters

    Focus on *how* and *why* not *what.*

Personal Reflection:

Pick a random scene from your latest piece. Score the vividness of your emotions on a scale of 1-5 with 5 being extremely intense.

Then give that scene to a beta reader (can be a friend or family) that reads frequently. Ask him/her to score the emotion using the same scale. How similar is your rating?

Taking that same scene into consideration, what can you do to "ramp up" its emotional viability?

CHAPTER 6:

Keeping *history* in your story

We began by talking about how important history is to our world and I'd like to end on that same note. But this time, I'd like to focus on the problem that confronts every historical author but is most common to writers of fiction.

What do we do in those moments where our plot isn't exactly... historical?

Writers are creators. As such, we transcend the realities of history—at least in our minds. But the truth is that we need to always maintain the balance between the *historical* and the *fiction.*

When we give history a makeover, we lose credibility with our readers, we detract from our book's educational value and—worst of all—we run the risk of losing sight of the past.

If you are writing a non-fiction piece, such as a biography, please just give us the facts as they are under the umbrella of your unique writing ability!

That being said, it is more important to capture the *feelings* of a society—on *all* sides of an issue—than it is to relate historical facts.

Here are a few practical options to help you navigate this literary Scylla and Charybdis.

Create a historical alter/ego

Many contemporary readers are familiar with the work of Joel Rosenberg, author of *The Kremlin Conspiracy* and other political thrillers. Rosenberg's work sometimes includes fictional characters that are based off of real people. The character's traits, personal habits and political decisions allow readers to make a connection in their minds between the fictional character and the real person that inspired that character.

In a similar manner, historical authors should consider creating a fictional character whose major decisions are reflected in the historical record but whose personal life they can manipulate to better suit the plot.

Include an author's note

An author's note that addresses the historical liberties taken by the author can prevent misinformation or—equally distressing—negative reviews about failed historical accuracy.

Clue your readers in to the fact that what they have read, or are about to read, has some modifications to the historical record. Personally, I go as far as to identify the major disparities and then present my readers with the facts.

Use alternative history

I use historical fiction as an opportunity to teach spiritual and moral truths. With that in mind, if I know that my point won't be made without a dramatic (but logical) alteration to the historical record, I inform readers that this is a work of alternative history.

Being candid with readers is always best. Considering labeling your work as alternative history does not detract from the research or the historical relevance as the setting, events and the details we mentioned earlier will, no doubt, find their place in the epoch you're writing about.

Fake people, real setting

In a slight variation of the above, a historical fiction author may want to simply invent a cast that is not linked to real individuals but represent an entire social group in a real setting.

This approach probably gives fiction writers the most leeway as the author isn't pigeon-holed by details that may be in a historical person's life but don't suit the plot.

Constructive destruction

If none of the above meet your needs, then it is time to consider the inevitable: an adjustment of your plot. While I realize that no author wants to consider changing what he or she has envisioned, sometimes that is the only feasible approach—and it is one that can only make you a better writer.

Takeaway:

1. Bending history should be avoided when at all possible. It should never happen in biographical or non-fiction pieces.

2. For fiction, there is a little more room for grace (it is *fiction* after all) but, unless readers are aware that they are picking up a work of alternative fiction, keep the historical modifications to a minimum.

3. Good historical writers focus on capturing the feelings of a historical era—not just the facts.

4. Some strategies to keep faith with your readers include:

    - Creating a fictional person that's inspired by a real one.

    - Include an author's note or introduction that identifies the elements of history that you've changed.

- Write a novel that is explicitly alternative history.

- Put completely fictional people in a historical setting.

- Adjust your plot to better suit the historical record.

Personal Reflection:

1. Do you believe that preserving the historical accuracy in fiction is important? Why or why not?

2. How has reading this chapter impacted your view on the importance of changing historical events?

3. Analyze your latest manuscript. Did you take any historical liberties? Make a list then compare that list to the historical *accuracies* your piece contains. Which is greater in number?

Conclusion

I truly hope that the information presented in this guide is helpful. Writing history is certainly not for the faint-hearted. After reading this workshop-in-a -book you may wonder if you have what it takes to produce a masterpiece.

You do.

Like most things, authors improve with time. Don't be discouraged if your manuscript or your recently published work doesn't quite fit all of the descriptions outlined above. Collaborate with other authors, continue to write and revise what you have already written.

Rethink. Revise. Reinvent.

Such is the lifecycle of civilizations—and of authors.

A note from the author:

I gave my heart to Jesus Christ as a kid and, I have to say, it was the best decision I've ever made. He gave me purpose, and kept me on the right path in a tough school and challenging home environment. Almost thirty years later, I'm proud to identify myself as a Christian.

My purpose now is to encourage others to find the same Source of inspiration. To that end, my wife and I've several works of fiction and non-fiction, some of which are listed below. In addition, my wife and I host a Christ-centered Facebook page, geared to helping married couples achieve a lasting, fulfilling relationship.

Check it out: **Facebook.com/FearlessMarriage**

If you haven't experienced the transforming power of Christ, reach out on the contact page of my author website: www.jprobinsonbooks.com. I'll be glad to share my story or do what I can to help you along the journey.

JP Robinson

IN THE
SHADOW
OF YOUR
WINGS
NORTHSHIRE HERITAGE BOOK 1
JP ROBINSON

In the Shadow of Your Wings (Northshire Heritage I)

Leila Durand, an elite German spy charged with infiltrating the home of British icon Thomas Steele, sees the war as a chance to move beyond the pain of st. But everything changes when she falls in love with Thomas's son, Malcolm. Is there a way to reconcile her love for Germany and her love for the enemy?

Thomas Steele sees the war as an opportunity for his profligate son, Malcolm, to find a purpose greater than himself. But when Malcolm rebels, it falls to Thomas to make tough decisions.

The war's reach extends to the heart. Eleanor Thompson finds her faith is pushed to the breaking point when her husband disappears on the battle front and her daughter is killed in a German air raid. Where is God in the midst of her pain?

In the Shadow of Your Wings presents inescapable truth that resonates across the past century. Then as now, the struggle for faith is real. Then as now, there is a refuge for all who will come beneath the shadow of God's wings.

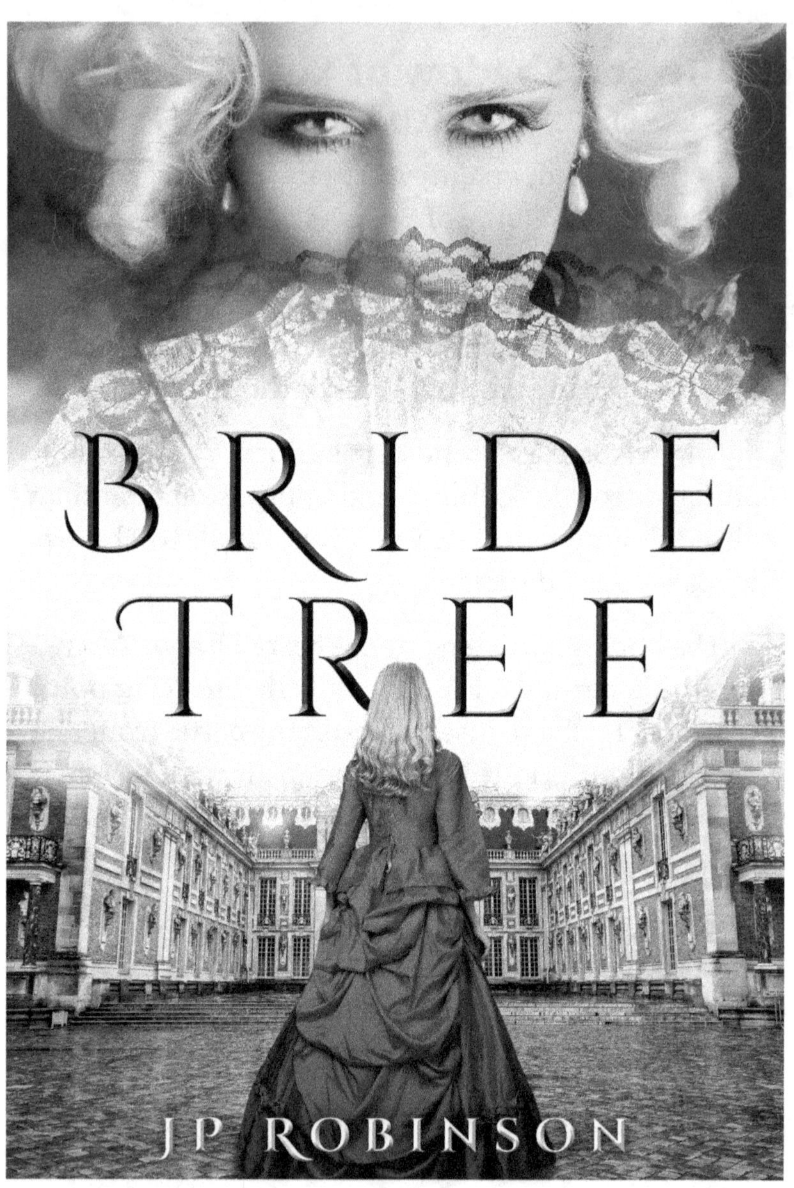

BRIDE
TREE
JP ROBINSON
SECRETS OF VERSAILLES II

Bride Tree
(Secrets of Versailles II)

UNMASK THE TRUTH

Bride Tree, a sweeping allegory of the Church set in the tumultuous French Revolution era, fuses alternative history with romantic suspense.

The year is 1789. France is reeling under the impact of a civil war between its social classes. When a secret agent from Rome joins forces with a vindictive politician bent on revenge, the stage is set for an explosive outcome that will shake the country to its core.

Meanwhile, Queen Marie-Antoinette engages the help of her lady-in-waiting, Viviane de Lussan, in a desperate battle to keep her throne… and her head. But how can she win a struggle she seems fated to lose?

Amid the chaos of the revolution, Viviane's heart is torn between a nobleman who sacrifices everything for her and a peasant who promises true freedom.

Twiceborn

Secrets of Versailles

Book 1

"I had a hard time putting it down." -Emma F., Reviewer

Twiceborn
(Secrets of Versailles I)

SOME SECRETS CAN KILL

Versailles is the center of European power but the court of King Louis XIV is also a hotbed of intrigue and political manipulation.

Despite the rigid structure of Angélique's upbringing, temptation proves stronger than her principles. She gives birth to twins, Antoine and Hugo, who are ripped apart by their mother's shadowed past.

Twenty-five years later, Antoine is caught in a web of intrigue when his jealous brother, now a powerful member of the clergy, accuses him of treason and threatens to destroy the woman he loves.

But Hugo has bigger plans than just his brother's downfall. He ignites a plot that threatens to bring the Kingdom of France to its knees, little suspecting the cataclysmic forces his actions will unleash.

Tears will fall, blood will flow and, in the end, only one man will remain standing.